Collins

My First Book of

Animals

Collins My First Book of Animals
Collins
An imprint of HarperCollins Publishers
Westerhill Road
Bishopbriggs
Glasgow
G64 2QT

First edition 2011
Second edition 2013

Copyright © Q2AMEDIA 2011

ISBN 978-0-00-752116-6

Imp 001

Collins® is a registered trademark of

HarperCollins Publishers Limited
www.collinslanguage.com
A catalogue record for this book is available from the British Library

Printed and bound by Imago in Singapore

Author: Sally Morgan
Editor: Jean Coppendale
Project Manager: Shekhar Kapur
Art Director: Joita Das
Designers: Ankita Sharma, Deepika Verma, Jasmeen Kaur,
          Kanika Kohli and Souvik Mukherjee
Picture Researchers: Akansha Srivastava and Saloni Vaid

For the Publisher:
Elaine Higgleton
Ruth O'Donovan

Managing Editor: Alysoun Owen
Editor: Jill Laidlaw

Collins

My First Book of

Animals

Contents

Animal World

Animals are found everywhere, from the tops of mountains to the deepest oceans, from scorching deserts to the frozen Arctic. Animals may look different but they are alike in many ways. All animals have to eat food to grow and to stay healthy. Many animals can move around, but a few spend their lives in the same place. In this book you will read about the lives of animals, the places where they are found and how they survive.

Giant pandas are mammals that live in China. They eat mainly one type of food – the shoots, stems and leaves of bamboo trees.

Brightly coloured monarch butterflies are a type of insect.

There are thousands of different types of bird, including this colourful toucan.

Crocodiles are large reptiles that live near water.

7

Types of Animals

There are many different types of animals. Some are covered in fur or feathers, others have a hard shell. Many have four legs, but others have two, six or many legs. Some animals have no legs at all.

Backbones

Animals can be divided into two main groups – vertebrates and invertebrates. Vertebrates are animals that have a backbone, such as fish, reptiles, birds and mammals, including humans. The backbone, or spine, is usually made of bone. The spine helps to support the animal's body and allows it to move around. Invertebrates are animals without a backbone, such as insects and worms.

There are six main types of animals: mammals, birds, reptiles, amphibians, fish and invertebrates, which are often called minibeasts.

Mammals are intelligent animals that are usually covered in hair. Most female mammals give birth to live young. They feed their babies milk.

Birds are covered with feathers and they have wings rather than arms. They have two legs and a beak with no teeth. They lay eggs with hard shells.

Nobody is sure how many different types of animals there are in the world. More than two million have been found and named, but millions are still waiting to be discovered.

Reptiles have scaly skin. Most have four legs but snakes, and some lizards, are legless. Reptiles lay eggs with a leathery shell.

Amphibians are four-legged animals that have a moist skin and live in or near water. They lay eggs, which hatch into tadpoles. The tadpoles change into adults.

Fish live in water and have fins rather than legs. Fish are covered in scales. They have gills that let them breathe in water.

Minibeasts, such as this beetle, are invertebrate animals. They live on land and in water.

Mammals

There are about 5,500 different types of mammals. Mammals include wild animals such as lions, monkeys and bears, domestic animals such as pet dogs and cats and farm animals such as cows and pigs. Humans are also mammals. The largest mammal in the world is the blue whale, a huge animal that lives in the ocean. It grows to more than 30 metres (98 feet) with a heart the size of a small car. The smallest mammal is the tiny bumblebee bat which is just 3 centimetres (1 inch) long and weighs about as much as a tea bag.

Many mammals live in groups called herds, such as these zebras in Southern Africa.

Wolves are the closest relatives of pet dogs. Wolves live in groups called packs.

Most mammals, such as macaques, take great care of their young.

Koalas are mammals that live in trees. They are found only in Australia.

What is a Mammal?

All mammals have hair, even whales. Most mammals give birth to live young, except mammals called monotremes, which lay eggs. Some baby mammals stay with their mother for many years, others for only a few weeks.

Keeping warm

Hair keeps mammals warm, so these animals have lots of hair or very little hair depending on where they live. Polar bears in the frozen Arctic have thick, white fur. Elephants live where it is very hot. They only have little tufts of hair on their head and at the end of their tail.

Polar bears have thick fur and a layer of fat that helps to keep them warm. Their feet have rough soles so they do not slip on the ice.

Baby care

Mammals look after their young. They feed them and teach them how to find food and survive. The young drink their mother's milk until they are ready to eat solid food. This is called suckling.

Orang-utans live in the rainforests of South-East Asia. The babies stay close to their mother for the first two years.

Wild and tame

Some mammals have been domesticated and are used to living with humans. For example, cats are now family pets, but they still share many characteristics with their wild cousins, such as lions and tigers.

Long life

One bowhead whale lived for more than 200 years, longer than any other mammal.

Cat life cycle

Cats are pregnant for about two months.

Cats give birth to a litter of kittens that feed on their mother's milk.

Cats can begin to have babies at about six months old, but it is better to wait until they are over a year old.

Kittens are ready to leave their mother at about ten weeks. Pet cats live for up to 20 years.

After about four weeks, the kittens start to eat solid food.

Big Cats

Big cats such as lions, tigers and leopards are members of the cat family. They are carnivores, which means they eat meat. They hunt other animals for food.

Teeth and claws

Wild cats have sharp teeth and powerful jaws to kill their prey. Their toes end in long, curved claws that help them to grip their prey so it cannot escape.

The canine tooth of a tiger can be up to 10 centimetres (4 inches) long. This is about the average length of a man's index finger.

Canine tooth

A pride of lions

Lions live in a group called a pride. A pride is made up of a male lion, several females and their young. The females do the hunting. When they catch and kill an animal, the rest of the pride comes to feed.

Cats pull in their claws (left) when they walk so they do not get worn down. Cats push out their claws (right) when they are ready to attack.

Jaguars may not be able to survive in the wild because the trees in their rainforest homes are being cut down.

Rainforest jaguars

Jaguars are large, spotted cats that live in the tropical rainforests of South and Central America. Like tigers, these cats love swimming and are often found near water.

Fast cat

Cheetahs are the fastest land animals. They can reach speeds of about 95 kilometres per hour (almost 60 miles per hour) in just three or four seconds. They can reach top speeds of 110 kilometres per hour (68 miles per hour).

Staying warm

Snow leopards live high in the Himalaya Mountains of Asia. It is really cold in the mountains, so they have thick fur to keep them warm. Snow leopards also have very thick tails that they wrap around their heads like a blanket when they sleep.

Snow leopards live alone. Their wide feet are perfect for walking on snow.

Monkeys and Apes

Monkeys and apes are intelligent animals that are quick to learn. For example, some of them have discovered how to make and use simple tools to catch ants and use leaves to collect water.

Monkey or ape?

Monkeys have tails but apes do not. Monkeys use their long tails to help them climb trees. Apes use their arms and legs to get up and down trees. Baboons, macaques and mandrills are all types of monkey. Chimpanzees, gorillas, gibbons and orang-utans are apes.

These woolly monkeys are using their tails to grip branches and swing through the trees.

Gorilla families

Gorillas are the largest apes. They live in family groups in the rainforests of Central Africa. Gorillas have big heads, large chests and very long arms. They are peaceful animals that feed on plants.

A family of gorillas is led by a male called a silverback. A silverback has a patch of silver-coloured fur on his back.

Snow monkeys

Japanese macaques or snow monkeys live in the mountain forests of Japan. The winters are freezing cold and some of the macaques have learned to bathe in hot water pools to stay warm.

Snow monkeys groom each other as they bathe. They warm up in hot water that comes out of the ground. This water is heated by hot rocks deep undergound.

Using tools

Chimpanzees have learned how to use twigs and leaves as tools to help them feed, drink and clean themselves. They poke a long twig into a termite nest. When they pull out the twig it is covered in termites, which they eat.

Howlers

Howler monkeys live in the thick rainforests of South America where there are so many trees it is difficult to see very far. They produce loud howls and whoops which can be heard more than 5 kilometres (3 miles) away. Some calls are warnings, but often they howl just to tell other monkeys "I am here".

Howler monkeys make most noise at dawn and dusk.

Hooves and Horns

Antelope, cattle, deer and horses are all types of hoofed mammals. They have four long legs and each leg ends in a hard hoof. Most hoofed animals are prey animals, which means they are hunted for food by other animals. Hoofed animals use their long legs to run fast to escape from predators.

Hooves

We walk on the soles of our feet, but hoofed mammals run on the tips of their toes, like ballerinas. Their toes are protected in a hard case called a hoof. The hoof is made of keratin, the same substance that forms our nails.

The hoof of this cow is split into two toes. Deer, sheep and cattle have two toes. Horses and zebras have hooves with only one toe.

Plant-eaters

Hoofed mammals are plant-eaters. Some graze on grass while others pull leaves off trees. Plant foods can be tough to chew so hoofed mammals have large, flat teeth which grind the food before it is swallowed.

Giraffes have long necks so they can reach leaves at the top of trees. They also have long, thick tongues so they can pull tasty buds and leaves from the branches.

Antlers and horns

Many hoofed mammals use their tough antlers or horns to fight and to defend themselves when being attacked. Male deer grow a new set of antlers every year. They drop their old antlers in the autumn and grow new ones in the spring, when they will need them to fight off rival males.

┄┄┄┄┄┄┄┄┄┄┄┄┄┄┄►

These two stags (male deer) use their antlers to fight over female deer. The stags may get injured but they rarely kill each other.

Nimble feet

Mountain goats live on the rocky slopes of mountains. Each hoof has two toes that spread out to give a better grip on narrow cliff edges.

┄┄┄┄┄┄┄┄┄┄┄┄┄┄┄►

To find plants to eat, mountain goats have to leap from rock to rock. They can jump more than 3 metres (10 feet) in a single bound.

Marine Mammals

Most mammals live on land, but whales, dolphins, seals and walruses are mammals that are found in water. Instead of legs, they have flippers that help them to swim. Although they live underwater, they still use their lungs to breathe, like other mammals.

Flipper

Dolphins can leap high out of the water. They do this for lots of reasons, sometimes for fun but also to escape enemies.

Dorsal fin

Slippery shape

Marine mammals have a fish-like shape that is good for swimming through water. Their tail ends in a pair of flat, rubbery lobes called flukes that help to push them through the water.

Tail

Fluke

Staying warm

Many whales live in the cold waters of the Arctic and Antarctic. Thick layers of blubber (fat) under their skin traps their body heat and helps them to stay warm.

Humpback whales feed on fish and tiny animals called krill.

Expert swimmers

Seals and sea lions are carnivores (meat-eaters) and eat fish and squid. They are clumsy on land, but in the water they can swim quickly and easily catch food to eat. Seals spend most of their time at sea, but the females have to return to land to give birth to their babies.

Young sea lion pups feed on their mother's milk, which contains a lot of fat. The babies become very fat to help them stay warm in the freezing water.

Risky hunting

Orcas, or killer whales, that live off the coast of Argentina hunt seals on the beach. They swim into shallow water to catch the seals and then use their powerful tails to push themselves back into deeper water. The adults teach the young orcas how to do this.

It is dangerous for orcas to hunt seals in shallow water. They may become stranded on land if they come too close to the shore.

Special Mammals

There are three groups of unusual mammals – bats, monotremes and marsupials. Bats are found all over the world, but marsupials and monotremes are found mostly in Australia and New Guinea.

Marsupials

Marsupials have a pouch, which is a flap of skin that forms a pocket. Their babies are tiny when they are born, so they stay in the pouch and feed on milk until they are large enough to come out. The best known marsupials are the kangaroos and koalas of Australia.

Monotremes

The duck-billed platypus and the echidna are monotremes, the only egg-laying mammals in the world. They lay one or two eggs at a time, which hatch into babies.

This kangaroo has a baby, called a joey, in her pouch. The joey stays in the pouch for about six months.

Echidnas are covered in fur and sharp spines. They have long claws that they use to dig for ants and termites. The young suckle on their mother's milk, just like other mammals.

Flying at night

Bats are the only mammals that can fly. They are nocturnal, or active at night. During the day, they hang upside-down in caves and under roofs, resting. At night they hunt insects and other small animals. They have poor eyesight and use sound to find their way around.

⋯⋯⋯⋯⋯⋯➤

The wings of bats are formed from their arms, with leathery skin stretched between long, thin fingers.

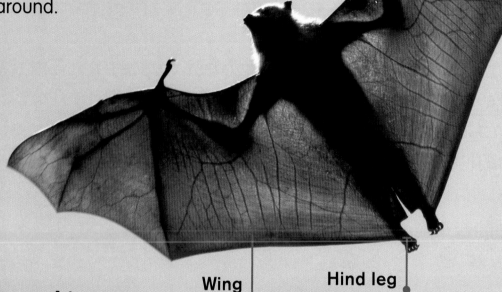

Finger

Wing

Hind leg

Dead or alive?

Virginia opossums are marsupials. Females can give birth to up to 20 babies at a time, but only a few of the babies survive. When threatened by a predator, these animals throw themselves on the ground and pretend to be dead.

This Virginia opossum is not really dead. It is just pretending to be dead.

Birds

Birds have wings and most of them can fly. This has allowed them to make their homes around the world. They have learned to survive in some of the hottest places on Earth, the deserts, and also in the coldest, the Arctic and the Antarctic. Some birds spend nearly all their time in the air, but other birds, such as ostriches and kiwis, cannot fly at all.

Birds come in many shapes, colours and sizes, but they all have wings, two legs and a body covered in feathers. All birds lay eggs, too.

Atlantic puffins are seabirds that feed on small fish. They have small wings that help them to swim as well as to fly.

These emperor penguins live in Antarctica. Penguins cannot fly but they are expert swimmers.

Scarlet macaws are a type of parrot. They are one of the world's most colourful birds.

25

What is a Bird?

There are about 9,000 different types of bird, big and small. The largest bird is the ostrich, which grows to be about 2-3 metres (6-10 feet) tall, while the smallest is the hummingbird, which is just about 5 centimetres (2 inches) long.

Feathered bodies

All birds have a body that is covered in short, soft feathers. These feathers help to keep them warm. Feathers also create a smooth body surface, which means a bird's body can move through the air more easily. Birds also have long, stiff feathers on their wings, called flight feathers, which help them to fly. A few birds cannot fly, but they still have wings.

Sit and sleep

Birds have two legs, which are covered in scales. Each foot has toes that end in sharp claws. Birds that perch on branches to sleep have four toes. The toes wrap around the branch and grip while the bird sleeps so it does not fall off.

Flight feathers are stiff so they do not bend when birds, such as this bald eagle, beat their wings.

Eggs in a nest

All birds lay eggs with hard shells. Inside the shell is a yellow yolk that surrounds the developing chick. Around the yolk is the egg white, called albumen. Most birds make a nest where the female lays her eggs.

Brightly coloured

Many birds are a dull brown colour so that they blend in well with their surroundings. Other birds, such as the macaw and the peacock, have very bright feathers. Many males are brightly coloured to attract a female. The female picks the male with the brightest feathers. The females are usually brown so they can remain hidden when they sit on their nest.

Each type of bird lays eggs in a certain size and colour. These eggs belong to a robin.

Male peacocks have amazing tail feathers that form a fan when they are spread open. They display their tail feathers to attract females.

Amazing Flight

Birds can fly because they have wings rather than arms. They flap their wings to fly. They have a lightweight body for their size so they can take off from the ground.

Wing shapes

Different birds have different shaped wings. Birds with long, broad wings can glide. This means they can travel long distances through the air without flapping their wings all the time. This helps them to save energy. They only flap their wings now and again to make sure they do not lose height. Fast-flying birds, such as swallows, have long, curved wings with pointed tips. This type of wing slips easily through the air and allows the bird to turn quickly.

Swallows have curved wings so they can twist and turn in the air to catch flying insects.

The albatross glides low over the ocean, dipping down to catch fish.

Acrobats

Hummingbirds are the acrobats of the bird world. They are the only birds that can hover, fly backwards and even fly upside-down. They hover in front of flowers and push their long beaks into them to get nectar. They beat their wings quickly, backwards and forwards, to stay in the same place.

•••••••••••••••••••••••••>

Hummingbirds beat their wings as many as 80 times a second. This makes a humming sound.

Clean and new

Feathers are easily damaged and become rough and out of shape if they are not looked after. Birds clean their feathers every day to keep them clean. This is called preening. New feathers grow once a year. The old ones moult or drop out and are replaced by new ones.

•••••••••••••••••••••••••>

Birds, such as this swan, preen their feathers with their beak to remove dirt. Swans also preen to spread a type of oil that their body produces over their feathers.

Fastest flight

The fastest bird is the peregrine falcon. When it dives to catch its prey it can reach speeds of up to 200 kilometres per hour (124 miles per hour).

Flightless Birds

The world's largest birds – ostriches, emus and rheas – cannot fly. They are too heavy to get off the ground. Other flightless birds include penguins and kiwis.

Large and fast

Ostriches may not be able to fly but they can run very fast. They are dangerous birds, too. They kick any predator with their powerful long legs. Unusually, the male also sits on the nest to incubate the eggs and cares for the young.

Ostriches can reach speeds of up to 70 kilometres per hour (43 miles per hour).

Cassowary

These odd-looking birds live alone in the rainforests of Australia and New Guinea. Cassowaries can be aggressive birds, attacking animals and even people that come too close. They feed on fallen fruit.

Antarctic survival

Adelie penguins and emperor penguins survive the extreme cold of the Antarctic winter. They have layers of fat under their skin and thick layers of waterproof feathers that prevent heat from leaving their body.

Expert swimmers

Penguins are great swimmers and use their paddle-like wings to move at speed through the water. They spend much of their life at sea, hunting fish. They return to land to lay their eggs and raise their young.

Cassowaries have a bony growth, called a casque, on their head. This protects their head as they crash through trees and bushes in the rainforest.

Penguins are clumsy on land but in the water they move quickly and gracefully.

31

Birds of Prey

Birds of prey are meat-eaters that feed on other animals. These birds hunt high in the air using their excellent eyesight to look for prey on the ground. When they spot something, they swoop down to snatch it up with their sharp talons. This group includes birds such as eagles, hawks, vultures and falcons.

The snowy owl lives in the Arctic, where its white feathers make it very difficult to spot in the ice and snow.

Excellent eyesight

Long, sharp talons for gripping prey

Powerful hooked beak for tearing meat

Worldwide eagles

Eagles live in almost every type of habitat, including deserts, coasts and mountains. Sea eagles and bald eagles are found in the Arctic, while harpy eagles live in the South American rainforests. The marshall eagle hunts over the grasslands of Southern Africa.

Eagles, such as this African fish eagle, take prey back to a perch where they rip it into pieces.

Eye spy

Vultures feed on the remains of dead animals that have been killed by predators such as lions. They spend the day soaring high in the sky on the lookout for a meal. Like other birds of prey, vultures have excellent eyesight and can spot food on the ground from over 6 kilometres (4 miles) away.

It is not long before a dead animal on the ground is surrounded by squabbling vultures and other scavengers.

Master fishermen

Ospreys feed mostly on fish. They watch for a fish swimming near the surface of the water and then they swoop down and catch it in their talons. The undersides of their toes are rough to help grip the slippery fish.

Ospreys can carry fish up to about 2 kilograms (4 pounds) in weight in their talons. This is the same as carrying two bags of sugar.

Life of a Bird

All birds lay eggs. The eggs have to be incubated, or kept warm, by the parent bird so the chick grows inside the egg. Some chicks are born naked and blind but others have feathers and can run around within minutes of hatching.

Chicks have a special tooth on their beak that they use to break out of the egg. This "egg tooth" falls off soon after hatching.

Courtship

Male birds have many ways of attracting a female. This is called courtship. Some call to females while others impress female birds by carrying out an acrobatic display. Often, male birds, such as the peacock, have brightly coloured feathers that they use to impress a female.

Japanese cranes do an amazing dance. They leap into the air, twist and turn, and bob their head up and down.

A haystack nest

Sociable weavers are birds from Southern Africa that live together in one huge nest. Groups of up to 300 sociable weavers build a nest that looks like a haystack hanging in a tree. Inside, there are lots of rooms and each pair lives in its own room.

Nest building

Most birds make a simple cup-shaped nest from twigs, grass and feathers. But others weave elaborate nests from grass, or use mud to make their nest.

Ospreys use twigs and seaweed to build nests that can be almost 2 metres (6 feet) across.

Life cycle

The female blackbird makes a small nest in which she lays three to five eggs. She incubates her eggs for about two weeks and then the chicks hatch. The chicks do not have any feathers when they are born, and they are blind. But the feathers soon grow.

The young birds are ready to leave the nest when they are two to three weeks old. The parent birds continue to care for their young for another three weeks before they fly away. Blackbirds live for about three years.

Parent birds build nests to lay eggs.

Birds usually lay three to five eggs in a nest.

Baby birds hatch out of the eggs.

Parents feed the babies until they are old enough to fly away.

Reptiles and Amphibians

Crocodiles and snakes, turtles and lizards all belong to the group of animals called reptiles. These animals like heat and they can survive in very hot, dry deserts. Only a few reptiles are found in colder parts of the world.

Frogs and toads are amphibians. They live on land but they have to stay close to water, where they lay their eggs. They have moist skin and are found in rainforests and other places near water.

Temple vipers and other snakes live in trees where they hunt for small animals.

Bright green tree frogs live in wet rainforests. The large sticky pads on their feet help them to cling to slippery surfaces.

Like all other lizards, iguanas are cold-blooded and sunbathe every morning to warm up.

Turtles are reptiles that spend most of their time in the water. They come to the surface to breathe, but they can also breathe through their skin.

What is a Reptile?

Reptiles are covered in scaly skin. Some have a hard shell. Most have four legs, but snakes, and a few lizards, are legless. Most reptiles lay eggs but a few give birth to live young.

Hard shells

Tortoises and turtles are reptiles with four legs and their bodies are covered by a shell. They do not have any teeth. Instead they have a beak, like a bird. They use their beak to chew their food.

Giant tortoises on the Galapagos Islands can grow up to nearly 2 metres (6 feet) long.

New tail

When attacked, lizards can drop, or lose, their tail, which wiggles on the ground to attract the attention of the predator (the attacking animal). This allows the lizard to escape. The lizard then grows a new tail.

Domed shell

Scaly leg

Beak

From beach to sea

Turtles live in water, but female turtles return to the beach where they were born to lay their eggs. They haul themselves onto the beach and dig a large hole. They lay their eggs in the hole and cover them with sand. A few months later, the baby turtles hatch and scuttle across the beach to the sea, where they spend the rest of their lives.

Eggs being laid

The life cycle of the turtle starts with the egg, which hatches into a tiny turtle. Turtles have long lives, some living 80 years or more.

Eggs hatching

Adult turtle

Hatchling hurrying to the sea

Sea snakes

Snakes are legless reptiles that have a small head and a long body and tail. Many can move across the ground with amazing speed. Snakes can also climb trees and some can even swim.

Sea kraits are snakes that live in the water. Their tails are flattened so they can swim quickly.

Slipping and Sliding

There are 2,900 different types of snake, from tiny water snakes to huge boa constrictors. Snakes live in deserts, forests and grasslands, in water and in our cities.

↑ Sidewinder snakes have an unusual way of crossing sand dunes in the desert. They move sideways over the sand.

Desert snakes

Deserts are places where there is little rain and daytime temperatures can be very high. Snakes are among the few animals that can survive in these tough conditions. Often they shelter in underground burrows to escape the heat.

Warning colours

Some snakes are very brightly coloured. These snakes often have a poisonous bite that they use to kill their prey. Their bright colours warn enemies to stay away.

Deadly snake

The most poisonous snakes in the world are Australia's inland taipans. Luckily they live in places where there are few people.

The red and black colours of coral snakes are a warning that they are dangerous and have a poisonous bite.

Squeezed to death

Constrictors are snakes that wrap their body around their prey so that the animal is unable to breathe. Once the animal is dead, the snake swallows it whole.

Snakes can open their jaws really wide so they can swallow large prey.

Hissing cobras

Cobras are poisonous snakes that live in warm countries, such as India. When threatened, these snakes lift their head and part of their body off the ground. They flatten their neck so that they look bigger. They make a loud hiss to warn the animal or person to stay away.

Cobras hunt rats, mice, frogs and even small snakes. Black cobras, like this one, grow up to 3 metres (10 feet) long. King cobras are even bigger and can grow up to almost 6 metres (20 feet) long.

Rattlesnakes

Rattlesnakes are dangerous snakes found in North America. They come out at night to hunt for small animals. They taste the air with their forked tongue to find out if there are smells of any animals around.

Fang

Venom

When a rattlesnake is ready to attack, it pushes its fangs forwards to bite its prey.

Lizards

Lizards are closely related to snakes. There are more than 3,500 different types of lizard and they make up more than half of the world's reptiles.

Iguanas

Iguanas look fearsome, but they are harmless plant-eaters. They spend much of the day basking in the sun. Other times, they rest in trees, where their green and brown colours help to hide them from enemies.

Sharp spikes for protection

Throat flap

Iguanas have a throat flap that they extend when they are threatened to frighten away enemies.

Komodo dragons do not chew their food, but rip it into large chunks with their powerful jaws.

Dangerous dragons

The world's largest lizards are Komodo dragons. Unlike iguanas, these big lizards are as dangerous as they look. They have a huge body, a long tail and a mouth full of sharp, jagged teeth. They wait for animals to come close and then leap on them or knock them over with their strong tail. They also eat dead bodies, which they can smell from several kilometres away.

Prey

Chameleons' eyes stick out and can swivel around so each eye is looking in a different direction at the same time.

Eyes

Changing colour

Long tongue

Odd-looking chameleons can change the colour of their skin to match their surroundings so they are not easily seen by enemies. They also change colour when they are angry. Chameleons live in trees and have a long tail that they wrap around branches. Their long, sticky tongue is rolled up inside their mouth. They flick it out quickly to catch insects.

Fingers and toes grip branches

Skin changes colour

Tail

Water walker

Basilisks are lizards that can run upright on their back legs. Young basilisks have even been seen sprinting across the surface of water if they are threatened.

Basilisk lizards live near rivers and streams in the Central and South American rainforests.

43

Crocodiles and Alligators

These giant reptiles have a large head with powerful jaws for grabbing their prey. They have a long body that is covered in thick scales, with four legs and a strong, spiky tail.

Lying in wait

Crocodiles and alligators lie in the water with just their eyes and nostrils showing. They wait for animals to come to the water to drink or swim near them. Then they leap forward and catch the animal in their powerful jaws.

A crocodile either swallows its prey whole or breaks it up into large pieces.

These crocodiles are gaping to keep cool. Animals have to be careful not to get too close as crocodiles can move quickly and attack suddenly.

Keeping cool

Crocodiles and alligators move in and out of the water to keep cool. In the morning, when it is cooler, they rest on riverbanks enjoying the sun. When they get too hot, they slide into the water to cool off. Another way of cooling down is to open their mouth wide. This is called gaping.

Swimming

Crocodiles and alligators use their long tails to push their bodies through the water. When they swim, they hold their legs close to the sides of their body. Crocodiles often sink and walk over the riverbed. They close their nostrils and do not breathe while they are under the water.

While swimming, crocodiles stick their legs out when they want to steer or stop.

Good mothers

Female crocodiles and alligators lay their eggs in a nest. They protect their nest, guarding the eggs from predators such as monitor lizards. The eggs take between two and three months to hatch.

Female crocodiles use their mouth to gently carry their young to the water.

All Sorts of Amphibians

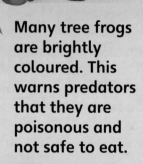

Frogs, toads, newts and salamanders are amphibians that generally live in the warmer places of the world, especially tropical rainforests. Most amphibians start life as fish-like tadpoles that generally live in water and move onto land when they are adult.

↑ **Many tree frogs are brightly coloured. This warns predators that they are poisonous and not safe to eat.**

Frogs and toads

Frogs and toads are small, dumpy animals with four legs. They live part of their lives in water and part on land. They feed on insects and worms.

Toads have heavy bodies and they crawl rather than jump.

Deadly beauty

Tiny poison-arrow frogs live in the South American rainforests. Their colours are amazing but they are also the most poisonous frogs in the world. Their poison oozes from their skin. Local tribes use the poison on the tips of their arrows to kill animals for food.

Poison-arrow frogs are not much larger than a thumbnail.

Desert survival

Spadefoot toads live in deserts. When the rains come, small pools of water form and the toads lay their eggs in them. These hatch into tadpoles, which have to change into small toads before the pools dry up. Then the toads burrow into the ground, where they live until it rains again.

Life cycle

Female frogs lay their eggs in spring. A clump of eggs is called frog spawn. The eggs hatch into legless tadpoles with long tails. The tadpoles have gills to breathe in water. Soon the tadpoles grow hind (back) legs and then front legs. Finally, their tails shrink and they become tiny frogs that can live on land.

▲ Spadefoot toads dig burrows using their spade-shaped feet.

Midwife toads

Some frogs and toads carry their eggs around with them. Female midwife toads lay their eggs in a long chain. Then the male toads wrap the chain around their legs and carry it around until the eggs hatch. This makes sure that the eggs are not eaten by predators.

It takes about three months for the eggs to hatch and the tadpoles to change into tiny frogs.

Spawn

Tadpole

Froglet

Adult frog

Fish and Other Water Animals

Two-thirds of the Earth's surface is covered by water. There are vast oceans, rivers, lakes and ponds. Many different types of animals live in water, but fish are the most common. Fish can be found in almost every watery place on Earth.

Coral reefs are home to some of the world's most colourful fish.

Other animals live in water, too, including this starfish, corals and sea urchins.

Jellyfish are found floating in all the world's oceans.

There are more than 24,000 different types of fish, including this butterfly fish.

Living in Water

Most fish have a smooth shape that slips easily through water. They have fins rather than legs and a tail that helps to push them through the water.

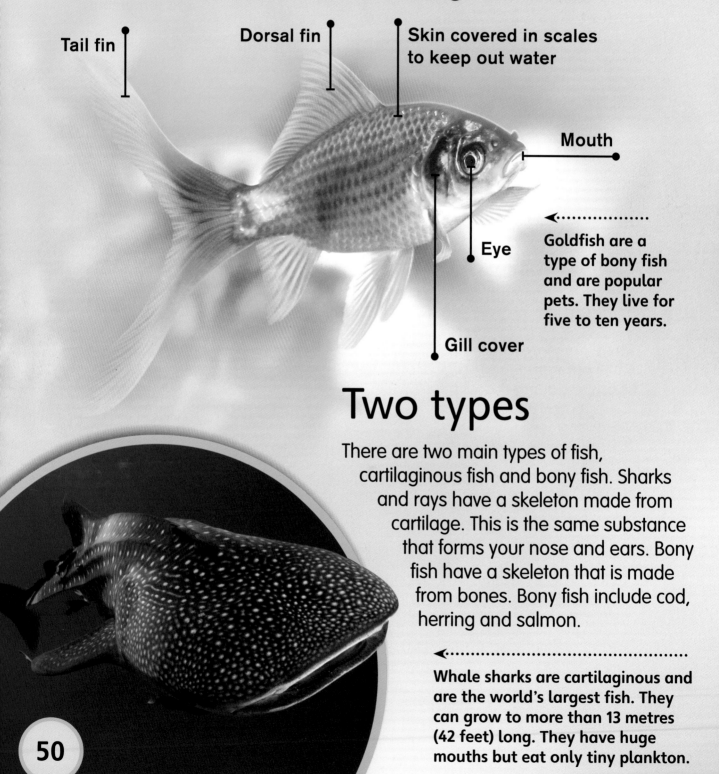

Tail fin

Dorsal fin

Skin covered in scales to keep out water

Mouth

Eye

Gill cover

Goldfish are a type of bony fish and are popular pets. They live for five to ten years.

Two types

There are two main types of fish, cartilaginous fish and bony fish. Sharks and rays have a skeleton made from cartilage. This is the same substance that forms your nose and ears. Bony fish have a skeleton that is made from bones. Bony fish include cod, herring and salmon.

Whale sharks are cartilaginous and are the world's largest fish. They can grow to more than 13 metres (42 feet) long. They have huge mouths but eat only tiny plankton.

Spot the fish

Can you see the fish hidden in this picture? Some flatfish, such as this finless sole, are perfectly camouflaged so that when they rest on the seabed they are almost impossible to spot.

Living in a shoal

Many fish live in a group called a shoal. Some of the largest shoals are made up of millions of fish. Fish are safer in a shoal than on their own because predators are confused by large numbers of moving fish–they are fooled into thinking a shoal is one large fish.

All the fish in a shoal move together in the same direction to confuse predators such as sharks.

Coral Reefs

Coral is alive and it is made up of many tiny animals that have joined together. Coral reefs are found in warm oceans where the water is shallow and clear. A dazzling variety of animals live on reefs, including brightly coloured fish, sponges, jewel-like anemones and fans of corals.

Building a reef

Coral reefs are built by many tiny animals called corals, which look like little flowers. Each coral animal has a ring of tentacles around its mouth. Corals come in a range of colours and shapes. Some corals are shaped like antlers, bubbles and tables, while others are shaped like fans.

Sea anemones look like plants but they are actually animals. They often attach themselves to coral reefs, where they wait to catch fish with their petal-like tentacles.

Mouth

Tentacles

Coral reefs are home to a quarter of all fish. Many have amazing colours and patterns.

Dangerous lionfish

Lionfish are easy to recognise with their striped body and fins that end in sharp poisonous spines. Lionfish are hunters. They use their large fins to trap small fish in a corner and then they swallow them whole.

················➤

If an animal or a diver swims too close, lionfish point their poisonous spines at them.

Disguised

Frogfish do not look like fish at all. Their bodies are shaped to look like pieces of coral. This makes it very difficult for predators to find them when they lie still on the reef. Frogfish can expand their mouth and their stomach to help them swallow animals up to twice their size.

Sea slugs

Sea slugs are related to garden slugs, but they are much more colourful. Their bright colours warn predators that they are not good to eat. Sea slugs eat reef animals that do not move, such as anemones and sponges.

Frogfish are brightly coloured so that they are camouflaged against the coral where they live. This means that frogfish can hide from both their predators and their prey.

Shark Attack

People are scared of sharks, especially the great white shark. But not all sharks are large or dangerous. Most sharks are quite small fish, only a metre (3 feet) or so long.

Shark features

Sharks have rough skin that feels like sandpaper. They have two wing-like fins just behind their head and a long, powerful tail that ends in a crescent-shaped fin.

A great white shark has about 300 serrated (jagged) teeth in its mouth, arranged in several rows.

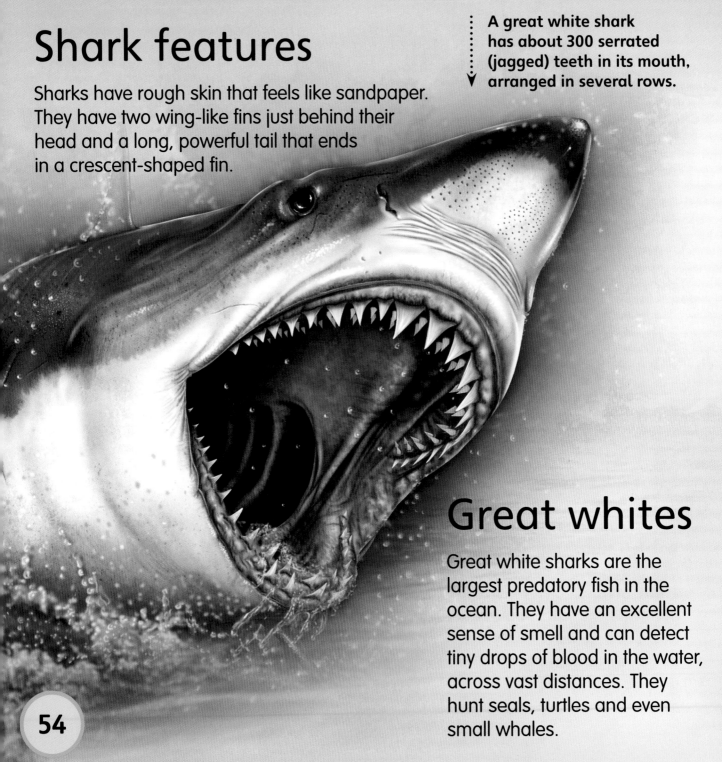

Great whites

Great white sharks are the largest predatory fish in the ocean. They have an excellent sense of smell and can detect tiny drops of blood in the water, across vast distances. They hunt seals, turtles and even small whales.

Ocean hunters

Sharks are predators and they use their excellent senses to find their prey. Seawater is often murky, so good sight is not important. Instead, sharks have a great sense of smell and taste. They can feel vibrations in the water, too. This helps them to find an animal that is swimming or splashing in the water.

Hammerhead sharks have a wide hammer-shaped head. Their eyes are at the ends of the hammer.

Eyes

Catsharks

Catsharks are small sharks that live near the seabed. Many have brown patterned skin, so they blend well with the seabed and are difficult to spot. They lay a small number of large eggs, and each one is wrapped up in a tough egg case called a mermaid's purse.

Egg cases are attached to seaweed so that they do not float away.

Baby sharks

Sharks grow inside an egg case for about six to nine months. When they leave the case, they look like small versions of their parents.

Catsharks get their name from the shape of their eyes. They look like cats' eyes.

55

Deep-sea Life

The deepest parts of the ocean are dark and cold. There is no light, so the animals of the deep cannot see anything. They use their other senses to find food in the darkness.

Sea monsters

There are many stories about boats being pulled into the deep by sea monsters with long tentacles. These monsters may have been giant squid, which grow to about 12 metres (about 40 feet) in length. Giant squid are fearsome predators that hunt large animals such as sharks and sperm whales.

Giant crabs

There are huge spider crabs on the seabed, with legs up to 4 metres (14 feet) long. Some live for 100 years or more.

Many sperm whales have scars on their bodies from their fights with giant squid.

New life

Scientists have discovered some strange animals that live at the bottom of the deepest oceans. These creatures are found around cracks on the seabed where hot water pours out. Giant tube worms, crabs and mussels are found near these cracks, which are not found anywhere else.

←··

These giant tube worms grow to more than 1 metre (3 feet) long.

Fishing fish

Anglerfish have a long spine sticking out of their head. At the end of the spine is a glowing light. They can dangle this light in front of their mouth. Other fish swim towards the light and are swallowed by the anglerfish.

Glowing light

Spine

Huge mouths

There is very little food in the deep ocean and fish may wait months before they find something to eat. Deep-sea fish, such as gulper eels and viperfish, have extra-large mouths and big stomachs so they can swallow almost anything that comes close.

Anglerfish have dagger-like teeth which they use to grip their slippery prey.

Minibeasts

There are far more invertebrates, animals without a backbone, in the world than vertebrates. These invertebrates are called minibeasts, and they include insects, spiders, worms and snails. Insects are the most successful animals of all. There may be as many as ten million different types of insects.

Most insects, such as these butterflies, have wings, so they have been able to spread around the world.

Shimmering dragonflies live near water, where they give birth to their babies.

Centipedes have a pair of legs on each body segment.

Crabs are crustaceans and have a heavy shell that protects their body.

59

What is a Minibeast?

Minibeasts are grouped according to their appearance, for example by the number of body parts, legs or wings they have. Insects such as bees and butterflies have six legs. Spiders and scorpions have eight legs. Crabs have ten legs. But slugs, snails and worms have no legs at all.

Millipedes are arthropods. The word millipede means a thousand legs, but the most any millipede has is about 750 legs.

Jointed legs

The largest group of minibeasts are the arthropods. These animals have jointed legs that can bend and bodies covered in a tough outer covering. There are lots of different types of arthropods, including spiders and crabs.

Stag beetles grow to about 5 centimetres (2 inches) long. The males use their antler-like jaws to fight other males.

Crabs

Crabs have eyes on the ends of two stalks called antennae. They have ten legs, five on each side of their body. The first pair of legs ends in large claws called pincers. Crabs use their sharp pincers to pick up food and to fight other crabs and predators.

Most crabs live in water, while others live on land. Some, like this coconut crab, can even climb trees.

Snails have a head with two pairs of tentacles that they use to tell them about their surroundings.

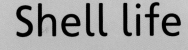
Tentacles

Shell life

Molluscs are soft-bodied animals that usually have a shell. Garden snails have a single shell that covers their soft body. They crawl over the ground on their fleshy foot. When threatened, snails pull their head into their shell for protection.

Wiggly Worms

Worms have a long, soft body and no legs. They do not have a proper head. Their body is divided up into sections, called segments.

Worm homes

Many worms live in the soil, such as earthworms and nematodes or roundworms. Fan worms and ragworms live in the sea. Tapeworms and many types of roundworms live inside other animals.

Fan worms live in a tube on the seabed. They have sticky tentacles that they use to catch tiny animals.

Wonder worm

The longest known earthworm was found in South Africa. It was nearly 7 metres (23 feet) long! The longest garden earthworms are only about 30 centimetres (12 inches) long.

Earthworms

Earthworms push their way through the soil. They feed on soil and dead leaves, which they pull into their burrow to eat. Any food not used passes out of their body and is left as a pile on top of the soil. This is called a worm cast.

Earthworms can regrow part of their body. If a bird pulls a worm in half, the front half grows back into a new worm.

Tapeworms use their hooks and suckers to grip the wall of the gut.

Tapeworms

Tapeworms are parasites. These are animals that live in or on other animals and do them harm. Tapeworms have a long yellow-white body made up of many segments. They have a head with hooks and suckers, but they do not have any eyes. Tapeworms live in the gut of other animals where they feed on food passing down the gut. They harm the animal by starving it of food.

63

Butterflies and Moths

Butterflies have wings in amazing colours. They are active during the day, when they fly from flower to flower in search of nectar. Moths are not so brightly coloured and are mostly active at night.

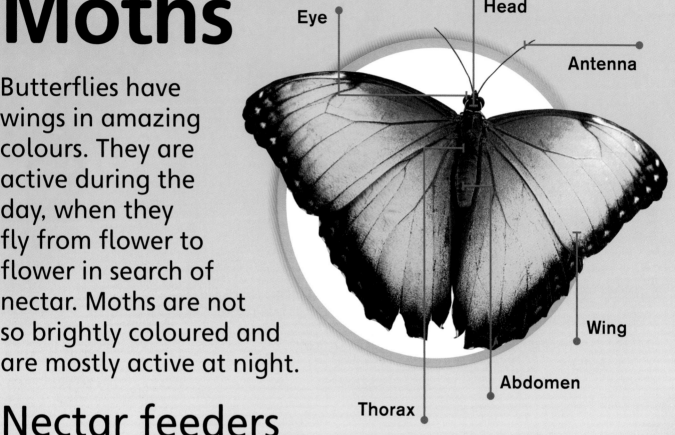

Eye

Head

Antenna

Thorax

Abdomen

Wing

Nectar feeders

Butterflies and moths are liquid feeders. They do not have jaws. Instead, they have a long tube at the front of their head called a proboscis. They push this into flowers to suck up the sugary nectar.

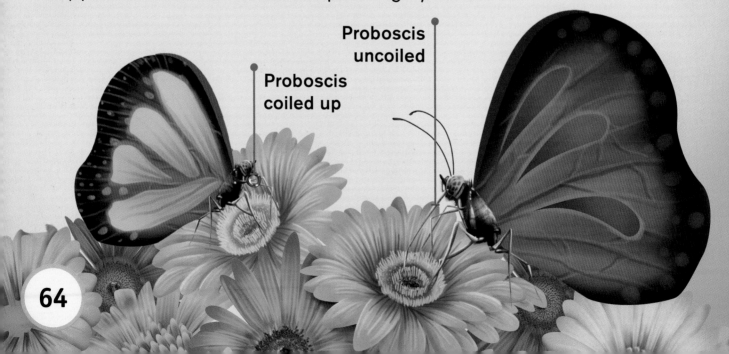

Proboscis uncoiled

Proboscis coiled up

Life cycle

The life cycle of butterflies starts with female butterflies laying small round eggs on a leaf. The eggs hatch into caterpillars. Caterpillars have a long, round body with segments. Caterpillars eat leaves and grow, and soon turn into pupae with a shell-like covering. Inside a pupa, the body of the caterpillar changes into an adult butterfly. This can take many months. The pupa splits open and the new adult emerges.

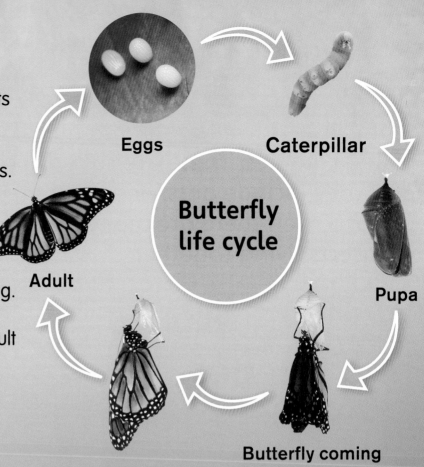

Eggs

Caterpillar

Butterfly life cycle

Pupa

Adult

Butterfly coming out of the pupa

Butterfly or moth?

Butterflies are usually brightly coloured and fly during the day, while moths are less colourful and fly at night. But there are a few brightly coloured moths, too. Butterflies have long antennae with a knob at each end, while many moths have antennae that look like tiny feathers.

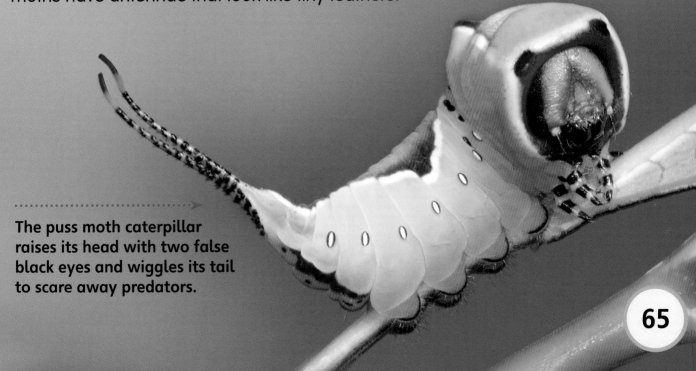

The puss moth caterpillar raises its head with two false black eyes and wiggles its tail to scare away predators.

Living Together

Many insects live together in huge groups called colonies. These are called social insects and they include ants, bees, termites and wasps. Often there are many millions of insects living together.

Workers, drones and queens

In a colony of honey bees there are three types of bee. Most honey bees are worker bees. These are the female bees that build and guard the nest, look after the young bees and collect nectar and pollen. Drones are male bees and their only job is to mate with the queen. There is one queen bee, an extra-large bee that lays all the eggs.

Queen bee

The queen bee can lay up to 1,000 eggs a day.

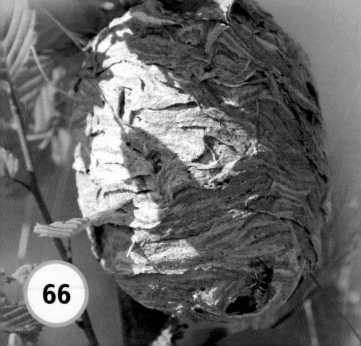

Paper nests

Wasps make their nests from chewed bits of wood, bark and paper. They chew the pieces into a paste, which they use to make the walls of their nest. The paste hardens in the sun.

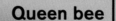

This wasp nest is about the size of a soccer ball. It could be home to thousands of wasps.

Army ants

Army ants live in rainforests and they are very fierce. Each day, millions of army ants swarm across the forest floor looking for food. A swarm may catch as many as 100,000 small animals on a day's hunt.

Tiny ants

Pharaoh ants are so small that 100,000 of them would weigh just 1 gram (0.03 ounce).

It may take a colony of termites as long as 50 years to build a home that is several metres or feet high.

Termite mounds

Termites are small, blind insects that make amazing homes that rise from the ground like columns. The walls are made from mud stuck together with saliva. The home goes deep into the ground, where there are many underground rooms.

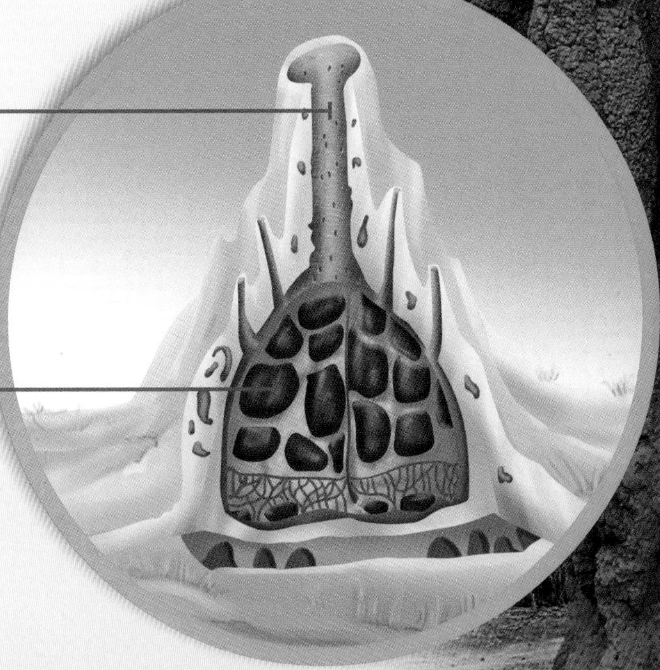

Air shaft

Underground rooms

Spiders

Spiders are hairy animals with a small body and eight long legs. All spiders can bite, but only a few have a deadly bite that can kill. Most spiders are harmless. Spiders produce silk threads that they use to make webs.

Body parts

Spiders have a body made up of two parts. The front part is the head-thorax and the back part is called the abdomen. Spiders are covered in hairs which help them to feel vibrations, tiny to and fro movements in the ground.

Tarantulas are also known as baboon spiders in South Africa because their legs look like baboon fingers. They live in underground burrows.

Leg

Head-thorax

Abdomen

Sticky webs

Orb web spiders make a web to catch their prey. The web is made from silk threads. The spider lies in the centre of its web, or hides nearby, and waits for an insect to fly into it. The insect gets trapped by the sticky silk and is grabbed by the spider.

Trapdoor spiders

These spiders do not make a web, but live underground in a burrow. The entrance to the burrow is hidden by a trapdoor. The spider waits at the entrance, with the door partly open. When a prey animal passes close by, the spider leaps out and pulls it into its burrow.

This wasp spider has wrapped up its prey in silk. It may eat it weeks later.

Poisonous bite

Spiders have needle-like fangs that can pierce the body of their prey. When they bite, poison runs down their fangs into the animal's body. The poison does not kill but it paralyses the animal so it cannot move. Spiders like fresh meat, not dead meat, so they wrap up the live animal in silk thread and eat it later.

Spiders have up to eight eyes and a pair of jaws that hang beside their mouth.

Eyes

Jaws

Saving Animals

Once there were vast wild areas in the world where animals roamed. As the number of people on Earth grows, these wild areas disappear. There are not many places left that are untouched by people. The survival of many animals, such as lions, giant pandas and whales, is under threat if we do not do something to save them.

Oil is transported around the world in tankers. When accidents happen, oil spills into the oceans, where it harms many animals. This pelican is covered in oil after an oil spill.

Plastic bottles and other rubbish often end up in rivers or washed up on beaches.

Animals disappear when their homes are destroyed. Huge areas of rainforests have been cut down.

This sperm whale is being hunted in the Atlantic Ocean. Many species of whales have been hunted so much that they have become endangered.

Animals in Danger

Animals are in danger for many reasons, but most threats to animals are caused by people. Animal homes have been destroyed by people. Many animals are hunted for their horns, tusks, meat and skin.

Vanishing rainforest

Rainforests are home to more animals than any other type of habitat. But more than half the world's rainforests have disappeared. The trees have been chopped down and the ground cleared for farming or to dig valuable rocks from the ground.

Leopard and crocodile skins were used to make coats, shoes and bags.

Land that was once forest is used for farming, new roads and homes.

Melting ice caps

People are burning more oil, coal and timber than ever before and this is causing the Earth to get warmer. The world's climates are changing, especially in places such as the Arctic. Polar ice is melting and sea levels are rising. This floods low-lying land, leaving people and animals homeless.

Polar bears get stranded in the Arctic when the ice starts to melt earlier than usual.

Gone forever

One in every five types of mammal, one third of amphibians and one quarter of reptiles is under threat of disappearing forever if we do not do something to save them.

Millions of sharks are hunted for their fins. The fins are cut off and hung out to dry for shark fin soup.

Overfishing

Too many fish are being caught and not enough are left to breed and produce more fish. Sharks are caught too, just for their fins. In many places sharks have disappeared and the survival of others is under threat.

Helping Animals

Fortunately, many people care about animals and there are ways that we can help to save them. Animal homes can be protected and new homes made for them. You can learn why it is important to save animals.

Safari parks

Places where animals live can be protected by making them national parks or nature reserves. This stops people from hunting the animals or clearing the land for new homes or roads. People can visit protected places to watch animals.

These tourists are watching elephants in a national park. There are many parks like this in Africa.

Animal tourism

Many people travel to Africa to watch animals such as elephants and rhinos. If these animals are protected, the local people will earn money from the tourists. If the animals are killed, there will be no tourism and no more money.

Stop the poachers

Many animals are killed because their horns or tusks, skin or fur are valuable and can be sold for a lot of money. This is called poaching. There are laws to stop this but the trade still goes on. People can be taught that it is wrong to kill animals in this way.

·····································>

Many rhinos are killed for their horn. One way to protect rhinos is to cut off their horn. This does not hurt the animal and it means that the poachers leave them alone.

Success story

Some animals have been saved. The California grey whale was hunted until it almost disappeared. Hunting of these whales stopped in 1946. Since then their numbers have increased. Now this whale has been taken off the "at risk" list. Hopefully, other animals can be saved, too.

·····································>

Watching grey whales is very popular in California and Mexico.

Useful Words

abdomen The hind part of the body of an animal such as an insect or spider.

amphibian A vertebrate animal that lives part of its life in water, part on land, for example frogs, toads and newts.

antenna Feelers on the head of many invertebrate animals, such as insects and crabs, that are used for sensing.

arthropod An invertebrate animal with a tough outer covering and jointed legs.

bask To lie in the sun to get warm.

bone A structure made from hard, white material that forms the skeleton of an animal, such as a mammal or bird.

burrow A tunnel in the ground dug by animals.

canine (tooth) A large tooth found near the front of the mouth. The canine tooth is long and sharp in predators such as big cats.

cartilage A substance found in the body of animals, for example the nose and ear.

cold-blooded An animal that uses heat from its environment to keep its body warm.

colony A large group of animals living together, for example bees and termites.

crescent-shaped Curved, shaped like a new moon.

desert A place that gets very little rain, has few plants and is often very hot during the day, for example, the Sahara Desert in North Africa.

domed Having an upside-down bowl shape.

domesticated An animal that has been tamed and is used to living with people, for example dogs, cats and horses.

endangered An animal that is at risk of becoming extinct and disappearing forever.

fang A long, pointed tooth.

feather A structure made from keratin that grows from the skin of birds and covers their body.

gills The parts of a fish that they use to breathe in water.

gut The intestines of an animal, where food is digested.

hover To stay in one place in the air.

incubate To keep warm.

jointed Having a limb that can bend at certain points.

keratin The tough material that forms hair, fingernails and hooves.

marsupial A type of mammal that keeps its young in a pouch, for example a kangaroo.

murky Not clear, dark and gloomy.

nectar The sugary liquid produced by flowers.

nimble Able to move quickly and easily.

nocturnal An animal that is active at night, for example badgers.

paralyse To prevent an animal from being able to move.

parasite An animal that lives on or in another animal, causing it harm, for example tapeworms that live in the gut of many animals.

poisonous Harmful and sometimes deadly.

polar ice Thick ice in the Arctic and Antarctic.

pollen Yellow dust-like particles produced by flowers.

pouch A pocket that a female marsupial has where it keeps its baby.

plankton Tiny plants and animals found floating in the upper layers of oceans, lakes and ponds.

predator Animal that hunts and eats other animals.

preen When a bird smooths, straightens and cleans its feathers with its beak.

prey Animal that is hunted by other animals.

proboscis A long tube used for sucking up liquid food, for example butterflies have a long proboscis that can be coiled up when not in use.

pupa The final stage in the life cycle of an insect when the larva changes into the adult.

rainforest Thick, evergreen forest or jungle found in warm places where it rains a lot.

saliva The liquid produced in the mouth to make it easier to swallow food.

scaly Skin that is covered in scales.

scar A mark left by a wound after it heals.

scavengers Animals that feed on the remains of dead animals and plants.

serrated Having a sharp, jagged edge.

shoal A group of fish.

spine The backbone of an animal.

sucker A structure that sticks to surfaces or to the skin of animals, found on the tentacles of the octopus and on the head of a tapeworm.

suckling A young animal drinking milk from its mother.

swarm A large group of animals, usually insects.

swivel To turn around from a certain point.

talon The sharp claw of a predatory bird such as an owl or eagle.

tentacle A long, flexible arm-like structure on invertebrates such as sea anemones and squid.

thorax The middle of the main divisions of the body of an animal, such as an insect or a spider.

venom A poisonous substance that some animals, such as snakes and spiders, put into other animals by biting or stinging.

Index

Picture Credits

t=top, c=centre, b=bottom, tr=top right, tl=top left, tc=top centre, cr=centre right, cl=centre left, br=bottom right, bl=bottom left.

Cover: © **Shutterstock.com**: ANP

Title Page: © **Shutterstock.com**: ANP

Half Title: © **Shutterstock.com**: ANP

Contents Page: **Thinkstock**: Ablestock.com/Getty Images, Jupiterimages/liquidlibrary/Getty Images, Tom Brakefield/Stockbyte; **Bigstock**: Joseph DeStazio, Hiroyuki saita, Elena Elisseeva; **iStockphoto**: Martin Strmko

Inside:

AP Photo: Charlie Riedel P70-71; **Bigstock**: Alexandr Tujicov P6; Emily Mills P7(c); Serge Vero P8(l); Hongqi Zhang P9(cl); Johannes Lodewikus van der Merwe P10-11; Anita Huszti P11(t); Eric Gevaert P11(c); Liv & Aaron Whitford P11(b); Yan Gluzberg P14; Stephen Meese P15(t); Neale Cousland P17(t); Gina Smith P18(t); Rob Gubiani P22(l); Sandra Caldwell P22(r); Jan Martin Will P25(c); James Chagares P26-27; Chan Yee Kee P27(b); Uryadnikov Sergey P32; Eric Isselée P33(t); Vadim kozlovsky P34(t); Kraska P36; Dan Exton P39(r); Andrew Potter P39(bl); John Pitcher P41(c); Eric Isselée P42(t); Pius Lee P42(b); Duncan Noakes P44(t); Melanie DeFazio P46(c); Levent Konuk P48; Victor Savsuhkin P49(b); Heidi Schneider P50(t); Arnon Wilson P52(t); Roman Vintonyak P52(b); Satori P53(t); Olga Khoroshunova P53(b); Teresa Gueck P60(t); Levente Varga P60(b); Holger Wulschlaeger P64; Laurie Barr P65(t); Nico Smit P68; Stéphane Bidouze P71(t); Jan Martin Will P73(t); Rob Gubiani P77(t); **Photolibrary**: Gerald Hoberman/Hoberman Collection UK P16(t); Pierre Huguet/Bios P39(tl); Roger Le Guen/Bios P39(tr); Guida Gregory/Bios P39(br); Martin Harvey/Peter Arnold Images P40(t); Gerard Lacz/Peter Arnold Images P43(t); Carol Farneti Foster/Oxford Scientific (OSF) P43(b); Michel & Christine Denis-Huot/Bios P44(b); Corbis P51(b); Morales/Age footstock P61(t); National Geographic Society/Imagestate P71(b); Christopher Swann/Bios P75(b); **Science Photo Library**: Thomas Marent, Visuals Unlimited P17(b); Nature's Images P47(t); Alexis Rosenfeld P55(c); Dr Ken Macdonald P57(t); Power And Syred P63(b); **Shutterstock**: Mishella P37(c); **Thinkstock**: iStockphoto P7(t); Jupiterimages/Photos.com/Getty Images P8(r); Jupiterimages/Photos.com/Getty Images P9(t); iStockphoto P9(cr); Ablestock.com/Getty Images P9(b); iStockphoto P12; Tom Brakefield/Stockbyte P13; Jupiterimages/liquidlibrary/Getty Images P15(b); iStockphoto P16(b); Anup Shah/Photodisc P18(b); iStockphoto P19(t); iStockphoto P19(b); iStockphoto P20(t); John Foxx/Stockbyte P21(t); iStockphoto P23(t); iStockphoto P24-25; iStockphoto P25(t); Gary Faber/Photodisc P25(b); Jupiterimages/Photos.com/Getty Images P29(t); iStockphoto P29(b); Stockbyte P30; Jupiterimages/Photos.com/Getty Images P31(b); Jupiterimages/Photos.com/Getty Images P34(b); Hemera P37(t); iStockphoto P37(c); Jupiterimages/Photos.com/Getty Images P46(b); Comstock P49(c); iStockphoto P51(t); Ablestock.com/Getty Images P58-59; Ablestock.com/Getty Images P59(t); Jupiterimages/Photos.com/Getty Images P59(b); iStockphoto P63(t); Hemera P65(t); iStockphoto P65(t); iStockphoto P65(b); Hemera P66(t); Jupiterimages/Photos.com/Getty Images P67(b); Hemera P69(t); Hemera P69(b); David Ponton/Design Pics/Valueline P72(b); David De Lossy/Valueline P74; iStockphoto P76; iStockphoto P77(b); **Getty Images**: Werner Van Steen/ The Image Bank P21(b); Andy Murch/Visuals Unlimited, Inc. P55(b); **Ecoscene**: David Manning P72(t); Mark Conlin P73(b); Luc Hosten P75(t); **iStockphoto**: Keng Iye cheok P20(b); Charles Schug P23(b); Jeremy Wedel P27(t); ChristianWilkinson P28(b); Sze Fei Wong P36-37; Nelic P41(t); Maria Dryfhout P41(b); Island Effects P45(t); Scott Leigh P46(t); Olga Khoroshunova P49(t); Island Effects P50(b); Enrico Boscariol P67(t); Luoman P71(c); Sze Fei Wong P78; **Fotolia**: Tanet Topradit P7(b); Nikolay Stoilov P28(t); Javarman P31(t); Bergringfoto P33(b); Erllre P40(b); Earl Robbins P55(t); Julien Scaperrotta P59(c); Tspider P61(b); Vilainecrevette P62; SibylleMohn P66(b); **Nature Picture Library**: Anup Shah P45(b); **National Geographic Stock**: Norbert Wu/Minden Pictures P57(b); **Mathew Field**: © Matthew Field, http://www.photography.mattfield.com P38; **Q2AMedia Art Bank**: 13(b); 14(br); 35; 36-37; 47(b); 54; 56; 64(b); 67(bl).